Discoveries
Along the Way
with Alan Thornhill

Susan Corcoran

ISBN 978-1-0980-7492-0 (paperback)
ISBN 978-1-0980-7493-7 (digital)

Christian Faith Publishing, Inc.
832 Park Avenue
Meadville, PA 16335
www.christianfaithpublishing.com

Printed in the United States of America

Foreword

My father, Alan Thornhill, was a priest, playwright, and a lover of people. These are the words my mother chose for his gravestone. Alan Thornhill was the son of an Anglican minister in a small Sussex town. Three of his four brothers were also ministers. Educated at Oxford and Wycliffe Hall, ordained in 1929 in Southwark Cathedral in South London, my father was on a trajectory to follow his father and brothers.

His life took a major detour when he met Frank Buchman and the Oxford Group while a student in Oxford. Buchman was an outspoken American who broke through the mustiness of Oxford academia and introduced many to a fresh and exciting new approach to living. He said to my father, "Alan, you need to read fewer books and more people."

This launched my father into a life full of people. He became a great listener. He developed an exceptional gift of friendship. He later wrote about many of these precious friendships in his book, *Best of Friends*.

This deep interest in people unexpectedly led him to play writing. While working with Buchman in America during the World War II, he wrote his first play, *The Forgotten Factor*. It was an industrial drama based on two families, one in management and the other the family of a labor leader. He drew on many of the people he had met through the focused work of industrial relations that Buchman and his team were engaged in. His habit of observing and listening (I often accused him of eavesdropping on those at tables near us in a restaurant!) and his gift of storytelling brought very real characters to life in his plays.

The Forgotten Factor played on Broadway and in Washington before arriving in London's West End. It was translated into sixteen languages and seen on all continents. Many other plays followed, including *Mr. Wilberforce, MP*, *Bishop's Move*, *Ride! Ride!* and *Sentenced to Life*.

When in the 1960s he retired to a life back in Sussex, he was asked to serve in the small country church in Mark Cross. He recognized this as a great gift and felt it completed the circle of his life. He often said there are not many people who could deliver the same message from the stage on a Saturday night and from the pulpit on Sunday. These reflections are taken from some of his sermons preached in Mark Cross.

In his last years, my father started a diary called *Discoveries*, full of insights, humor, observations from nature, and riches, mostly arising out of the many people coming to see him and what they said. He found something fresh almost every day. On December 2, 1988, just nine days before he died, he wrote, "I have a sense that something new and dramatic is going to happen. Is it my own death? Make the Advent message your own. Be alert. Watch. Get ready."

As I have edited these sermons, I have enjoyed spending time with my father. I realize what a great gift of faith he gave to me—a practical, down-to-earth faith that is less about dogma and more about relationships.

Susan Corcoran, Editor

Any Questions?

We like to ask questions and we like to hear people who may know more than we do, or who may not, try to give answers. We ought to ask questions. It is the best way to learn. This also applies to our faith and the Bible. People ask: "Is it up-to-date?" "Is it scientific?" "Who wrote it?" "What use is it?" All good questions. It is not wrong to question things, provided we do it honestly and remember that just because we don't understand or agree doesn't automatically mean that it isn't true.

But with the Bible, even more important than the questions we ask are the questions it asks us. I have been looking in the Bible for these questions.

The first one is in Genesis, the first book of the Bible. "The Lord God said to Adam: Where are you?" (Genesis 3:9). Adam and Eve were running away, they were in hiding. They were in a place of fear and shame.

The two most important questions on any journey are "Where are you going?" and "Where are you now?" Maps in parks or cities often have a big arrow with the words, "You are here." A friend of mine was lost in Ireland. He stopped and asked someone the way to Ballycroy. The fellow scratched his head and said, "Well, if it is Ballycroy you want, it is not from here I'd advise you to be starting." Like Adam and Eve we too can be hiding behind mental bushes—excuses, gripes, theories, bitterness, or frustrations—that stop us from seeing the truth about ourselves.

The next question is one that God poses to Eve: "What have you done?" (Genesis 3:13). It was asked of Eve because Adam had passed the buck. In our national discourse, it is so often the other person who is to blame. Wouldn't it be refreshing if someone dared to say, "Yes, we are to blame and we are sorry."

Some years ago, there was a famous conductor in New York who was suffering terribly with arthritis in his conducting arm. He went to a specialist who surprised him by asking, "Do you have any feuds or bitterness in your life?" As he faced these things and did everything in his power to clear them up, his arthritis was amazingly cured. I am not suggesting that all arthritis is due to feuds, but in many situations, the answer to a quarrel or a quandary may be the question, "What have you done?" A guilty conscience is a bad bedfellow. Honesty is often the best first step.

The third question comes in the next chapter in a story of two brothers Cain and Abel: "Where is your brother?" (Genesis 4:9). It is a good question for a race, for a nation, for an individual. The supreme test of life may be nothing about me, but what has been happening to the people around me. Cain, who had murdered his brother, made the classic reply, "Am I my brother's keeper?" That is the first question asked of God in the Bible. And the question still stands.

The key to life, to our nation's life, may be when we go humbly and honestly to God and ask, "Any questions?"

Very Powerful Holy Spirit

Two young women from Japan visited our church. I received a letter afterward from one of them. In it, she spoke of the great impression that our simple morning services had made on her. "I felt very powerful Holy Spirit."

A year later, I received another letter. She wrote, "I would like to tell you about what happened to me. After a wisdom teeth operation, I was suffering in great pain. But what was going on inside me was the pain of selfishness. I wondered how I could get rid of this sin. Then suddenly, Jesus spoke to me, 'I am the answer. Love me.' It was clear I should follow him. Nagasaki came to me as the place I should be baptized."

How the Holy Spirit comes to us is not our choice. We can't decide. If the spirit wants to come to us in some great dramatic experience, some wind or storm or fire, that is up to the spirit. It can happen. It happened to St. Paul (Acts 9:3–6) and many others since. But the Holy Spirit may choose to come to us quite differently. More like a whisper than a whirlwind.

My friend, the journalist and writer Malcolm Muggeridge, once described the presence of the Holy Spirit as "life in sync." You know what a film is like when the sound and picture are not in sync. It gives a strange, unreal, and confusing feel to everything. Now, life in this world for most of us is not in sync. We talk about being frustrated or confused. The times we live in are mostly out of sync with God. We live so much in reaction, in violence, and in breakdown.

When we open our hearts simply, very honestly, and humbly ask God and the Holy Spirit to take over our lives and release us from our selfish efforts and self-will, in a wonderful way, things fit. Life may still be difficult, there will be disappointments. But through it all, inside there is peace, there is a sense that it's all right, because God's spirit is with us and life is in sync.

I think of my Japanese friend who felt "very powerful Holy Spirit" in our church. That is why our church exists; for all who come, be they the most regular or the complete stranger, school child, or grandparent. It does not depend on the minister, it depends on us all. Who can tell how far the influence may spread? Perhaps as far as Nagasaki, a city once destroyed by the atomic bomb, now the setting for a new life in sync with the Holy Spirit. May we experience "very powerful Holy Spirit" together? The really important thing is that we as people move in sync. Let the Holy Spirit be a safety net for us. It is much more exciting, much more satisfying.

In the Beginning

"In the beginning God created the heavens and the earth" (Genesis 1:1–2). It doesn't seem to matter whether it was millions or even billions of years ago, whether it was a big bang or something altogether different. It still remains, "In the beginning God…" It is hard to think it is just an accident of atoms or blind chance. From the very start, there was a purpose and a meaning.

God says, "I am the Alpha and the Omega, the beginning and the end" (Revelations 21:6). We are part of this tremendous drama embracing the whole heaven and the whole earth. Can we see ourselves and our lives, precious beyond belief, following in the path of a mighty plan stretching back to the very beginning of everything and stretching forward to an even more glorious time that we can understand so faintly?

We live in a world of now, now, now with 24-hour news cycles, with crises piling on top of crises so that today's crisis almost makes us forget what last week's crisis was. The most common word we hear is pressure. So many younger people are overwhelmed by the rat-race, bowed down by this pressure that they feel like giving up. Perhaps we forget that our lives are but one hour playing out in the much larger panorama of history. God has a plan and we have a part. We just need to stop long enough and remember that we are privileged to have a small part in God's greater plan.

Some years ago, there was a young boy in a school not far from here who was under great pressure from his exams and life at school. Then his parents separated and his home broke up. His response was to set part of the school on fire. A friend of mine who counseled young people read about this story. He rushed to the court in Lewis and managed to persuade the judge to release the boy to his care rather than sending him to jail. In this different environment of care, the boy found a greater perspective than the pressure which had been overwhelming. He was able to gain strength and peace and grow up to play his part in God's greater plan.

God goes on to give us this promise, "To the thirsty I will give from the fountain of the water of life" (Revelations 21:6). We live in a very parched world. We know almost everything, but we believe almost nothing. We can be very dry in spirit. And then comes this great promise that God will give us what we need. It is interesting the condition he makes—not that we have to be good, not that we have to be worthy, not that we have to be deserving, not that we have to be wonderfully moral or holy. All we have to be is thirsty. He promises water from the fountain of life. Perhaps for many of us, water does not seem such a precious commodity, but if you live in a thirsty land like so many of the world's population, you know that when things become dry, they shrivel and die. Water is cool and refreshing, bringing everything to life. The water of life is a gift from God to give us life. It is encouraging that what we are offered is a constant fountain of living water that we can draw on every day.

A Heart of Flesh

Recently, I have been conscious of the disunity in our nation's life. Not that it is all that way. Sometimes with the screaming of the headlines and the ranting and ravings of various kinds of leadership, it is easy to forget that a depth of real unity exists. At the same time, we notice the tremendous sense of bitterness, of division, of violence, of vituperation, of real physical persecution, and all kinds of evidence of disunity—not just in politics and industry but also between races and generations and even between husbands and wives. What is the real basis of unity and what is our part? Indeed, amid labels and slogans and conflicting points of view, the thing that binds us together as one family is that we are all children of our heavenly father.

At a time of great disunity and bitterness, the prophet Ezekiel spoke this message from God to the Jews who were in exile, "I will give everyone one heart and I will put a new spirit within you" (Ezekiel 36:26). In the end, unity is a matter of the heart.

Unity is also a matter of the head. It is right that we should think out vitally important issues. Unity does not mean that we all think alike. There is room for variety and competition. But underneath all that, there is the unity of heart. Our great problems will never be settled until we deal with the human heart. So Ezekiel added, "I will remove your heart of stone and give you a heart of flesh" (Ezekiel 36:26). It's the hearts of stone that create disunity. Hearts that refuse to open and hear what is actually going on in the heart of the other person, the other group, the other nation.

A heart of stone can be turned into a heart of flesh. It may be very simple. I remember as a young man having to go and visit a friend and put right something that was wrong. It had started as something very small, but as very small things do, it had grown into something very big. This person lived on the third floor in the stone quadrangle of the college. I remember going up those three flights and every stone step was like a heart of stone crying out not to become a heart of flesh. I got to the top. I knocked on the door. There was nobody in. So I went down again. A second time, I went up the three flights of stone steps. I knocked again. Still nobody was in. I think God was trying to show me something about stone and flesh. And so the third time, I went up those steps slowly, step by step, three flights, and knocked at the door. There was my former friend. And as so often happens, when it actually takes place, it wasn't hard and we very soon became friends again. If we could all learn this simple thing, that unity begins with us. Unity in the end is a gift of grace. It is not something you just hammer out, it is something you have to receive with an open heart.

Build on Solid Ground

J esus was a trained carpenter. He knew something about building houses and what goes into them. When he spoke to the crowd about the new life that he came to bring to them, he described two houses. They look very much alike and you can't tell much difference between them. But they are very different because of the foundations underneath. When the sudden storms come, the wind swirls around, and water pours down, one of those houses stands firm, like a rock. In the other one cracks appear, water seeps in, the bottom crumbles, and finally, the whole house is swept away (Luke 6:46–49).

In the same way, there are two types of people. It may be hard to distinguish one from the other, but when the pressure comes, and it does come for all of us in little ways and big ways—perhaps it is a sudden shock or loss, a disappointment or surprise—there are some people whose foundations are firm. They know where to turn and how to stand firm. For others, there is no real foundation and cracks appear and life begins to crumble.

I know that every great dancer comes back to the same exercises every day because they know that unless the foundations are firm and practiced every day there will be a crash, a failure, and probably an injury. The great pianist Paderewski said, "If I miss one day of practice, I notice it. If I miss two days, the critics notice it. If I miss three days, the audience notices it." Behind every brilliant performance, there is a tremendous foundation of work and constant practice. A strong personal foundation also needs regular spiritual practice.

How do we get this firm foundation? Being like a rock doesn't mean being hard, being rugged, looking tremendously firm and strong. Not that. It is knowing where to go when things are difficult and when things are going wrong. Recently, I took a funeral for a woman who seemed to have a wonderful spirit of cheerfulness, of love, and a great sense of adventure. She spent much of her life in India where she was looking after the poor, doing an amazing job. Everyone said she was a wonderful woman with a strong faith and sense of service. To help me prepare to speak at the funeral, the family let me read her journal. All carefully written in long hand, it was a most interesting and honest account of all the battles that lay behind the apparent great faith. Sometimes, she wanted to die of embarrassment; sometimes, she was absolutely paralyzed with fear; sometimes, there were waves of jealousy and resentment against other people, and sometimes, she suffered great depression. The thing about her was not that everything was perfect and lovely but that whatever happened she knew where to turn. Jesus invites us to "come." At one point he says, "Come to me, all you who are weary and burdened, and I will give you rest" (Matthew 11:28).

Obedience to that call is the cement that holds it all together. Perhaps we have forgotten the importance of obedience. Once it becomes too difficult to obey, the foundations of our civilization begin to wobble and shake. But when we lay those true foundations, then whatever happens in the world, whatever storms, whatever floods come, we shall stand like a rock.

Absolute Perfection

Jesus commands, "Be ye perfect as your father in heaven is perfect" (Matthew 5:48). I was inspired to talk on this subject after watching the amazing performance of ice dancers Jane Torrville and Christopher Dean in the 1984 Olympics. When we see absolute perfection, it is not just about the gold medal, but it actually enriches life and makes it better. When it is joined with a certain modesty and gratitude to other people, it makes the perfection even sweeter. We often see it in art and music. There is perfection when we see spring burst forth or the stars in the sky at night. Sometimes, we experience something so amazing that as we go to bed we say to ourselves, "Well, that was perfect. That was a perfect day." These are glimpses of perfection. I think they help us realize what is possible and that in the mind of God, there is perfection. But then, part of the perfection is that we should be free people.

What does this mean in practical terms for us? I don't think it can mean that we are never to put a foot wrong, that we are to be so careful and so scrupulous that we do everything just exactly as it ought to be. There is something a little off-putting about that sort of striving after perfection for its own sake. Perfectionists can be wonderful people, but they can be a little tiresome!

Well, what does it mean? I think I learned something from the two classes of scoring by which they judge the Olympic skaters. First, there is technical merit. This is about measuring up to a standard. Life has standards. But a standard is not a standard unless it is absolute. If a pound weighs sixteen ounces one day but a bit more or a bit less at other times, it is not a standard. Measurements mean nothing unless they are absolute. We need standards.

The North Star is fixed in the heavens. Navigators have never reached the North Star, and never will, but through the centuries they have been able to know where they are, if they are off course, and how to get back on course again. We won't reach the North Star or absolute standards, but if that is how we set our course, we have a better chance of knowing when we are off course.

But then for the Olympic skaters, there is a second set of scores. They call it "artistic impression." This is a quality, an extra dimension that gives meaning. Perfection is not about never doing anything wrong but rather about adding something more to our lives. I think when we are told "Be ye perfect," it is a question of where you are going, where you are heading. Are you growing, maturing, and becoming more complete? Jesus gives this command in his Sermon on the Mount just after he has told them, "Love your enemies and pray for those who persecute you" (Matthew 5:44). Maybe this suggests that being perfect is especially in the realm of love. Jesus talks about loving the people who are hard to love and the people who don't love you. When people have treated you badly, when people have cheated you, that seems to be the place where love is really put to the test.

Maybe perfection is not just about individuals. It is a reminder that we need each other so that together as a family, as a group, as a community, we can grow into the fullness of what God would have us be.

Blessed Are the Pure in Heart

By far, the most valuable and revolutionary writings are the thoughts of Jesus as expressed in the Sermon on the Mount. They begin with the short sayings called the Beatitudes (Matthew 5:1–12).

"Blessed are the pure in heart for they shall see God." Can you imagine anything that cuts right across today's values or human inclinations than linking together happiness and purity? The advertisements, films, magazines, novels, plus the lives of people we read about in the tabloids, suggest that fulfillment is linked not with purity but impurity. "Blessed are the impure for they shall see life!" is drummed into us from every side day after day. Behind this idea are colossally important financial interests. Impurity pays big money and always has. If people are unable to say no to themselves, perhaps they will soon be unable to say no to violence or dictatorship.

What do we mean by purity? It is something more than rules and regulations or just a series of don'ts. Jesus did not abolish rules. There is a place for a few rules in life. But he went beyond them. Real purity is a positive. It is a passion. It is an affair of the heart. It is a great YES rather than a great NO. "You are to love the Lord your God with all your heart, with all your mind, with all your soul and with all your strength" (Matthew 22:37). That is purity, and the truth is there is not room in the human heart for both God and compromise. One or other has to go.

Once when I was traveling abroad, I got talking to a newspaper editor. He was full of the miseries, bitterness, and frustrations both in his life and of the world. I finally asked him, "What do you think is the key to the cure of all the misery?"

There was a long, long pause and then he removed a small latch key from his pocket.

"Well, perhaps this is the first key," he said, and without another word, he threw it into the lake where we were walking. It turned out it was the key to an apartment where every now and then, he paid illicit visits on someone. "I don't do it often, but I like to think it is there. But now, that is the end of all that!"

It was no accident that shortly after that the editor wrote and published an article that brought hope and enlightenment to thousands of people.

Purity is not an end in itself. Purity is the means by which hope and healing can come to the world. When a surgeon performs an operation, he first scrupulously washes his hands. He doesn't just go on washing his hands. He washes so he can begin the work of healing.

Finally, the result of purity is that we begin to see clearly. Sin of any kind blinds. It blinds us to other people and above all it blinds us to God. "Blessed are the pure in heart for they shall see God" (Matthew 5:8). A heart that has been swept pure of cobwebs begins to know God more clearly. Purity can be the most creative force in the world.

Breaking Down the
Wall between Us

Divisions are very real in every society in the world today. They go back to the earliest history of mankind. Often, it is a division between the privileged in society and those who feel they are victims of oppression. A wall of separation grows up between those who feel superior and snobbish on one side and those who feel angry and resentful on the other. These walls are not easily torn down. It is not as simple as forgetting the history that has created them. Words are not enough to end the enmity—the self-righteousness, the bitterness, the superiority, the remembrance of old hates, hurts, and grievances.

Now there is much talk about peace, and there is a sincere longing for peace in hearts everywhere. But there is a real danger that in talking about peace, we never get to grips with enmity, all that threatens and destroys our peace whether in our homes or whether it divides communities or countries. I think there is a danger that the great word "peace" can be taken and imprisoned and distorted by people of the left or right and used in absolutely false ways. We must find the way not just to talk about peace but to slay the enmity between us.

Let me share a personal story. When my wife, Barbara, and I were engaged and enjoying the thrill of the new relationship, there was a shadow over our lives. Barbara was working closely with someone who was a very strong-minded woman indeed. To tell you the truth, Barbara is no pushover either. Those two were finding it extremely hard to work together day by day. The enmity between them hung as a kind of shadow over our relationship. Every time we got together to think about our future, some new complaint and frustration came up. We talked about it, we sympathized, and sometimes we even prayed about it. Then one day, I met Barbara and her face was absolutely radiant, she looked quite different. I asked her what had happened. Rather casually, she replied, "Well, I just had one or two thoughts. Be ready to accept the whole blame. Forget the past, then expect a miracle, and let God pour in something fresh."

Do you know we never had to talk about it again? She never even had to talk to her colleague about it, but from that moment something happened, the walls came down and they forged a close friendship that lasted for years.

This is a simple example, but it is what St. Paul was talking about when he said, "For he is our peace, who hath made both one, and has broken down the middle wall of partition between us" (Ephesians 2:14). So as we pray for peace in the world, let us remember where peace comes from. He is our peace. It's not a question of "I'm right or he's right." But there is a third way when something new, something fresh, comes into a relationship.

A Famine in the Land

"See the days are coming, says the Lord God, when I will send a famine on the land. It will not be a famine of bread or water but of hearing the word of the Lord." (Amos 8:11)

I must confess that famine is not a thing that immediately leaps to mind when you are living in our western nations. The sheer impact of our supermarkets, the bewildering variety, the colossal quantity of every conceivable thing to eat, the huge bags loaded into our cars. The size of the servings in many of our restaurants can be overwhelming. There are even doggy bags to take the excess home. It doesn't make you think about famine. And yet of course, there is real hunger. As we look further afield, we can't help thinking about some parts of the world where there is terrible starvation. It is a strange world in which some of us are blessed with so much and yet others have so little. Millions in the world do not get enough to eat.

The Old Testament prophet, Amos, warned that the days of prosperity in Israel would come to an end. He was horrified at the luxury and the softness and the sheer corruption that he saw around him. So much of what he saw then applies to us today. The restlessness of young people wandering around having a good time, but somehow, there is a great hunger, a real malnutrition inside, not of things to eat but of finding a purpose in life. This great famine is really a hunger for knowing and hearing the word of the Lord. Who are the people who are really suffering from malnutrition? Not necessarily those who are the poorest but sometimes those who have the most.

I think there is a growing realization in many parts of our western world that we do lack an essential element in our spiritual diet. When I was recently in America. I was taken by my son-in-law to one of the big banks in Richmond at 7:30 in the morning to join a small group of a dozen men who meet together every week. This group is one of many across the country. It was a diverse group of bankers, lawyers, businessmen. and others who come together before work. I was impressed with the sense of relaxation. There was nothing pious about it. but there was an atmosphere where people felt very free to talk about what was on their mind. It was an honest conversation. Then we read together from the epistle of James, a very down-to-earth practical book. It includes a lovely bit about anger. Rob, my son-in-law, told them all of one really fierce row we had had early in our relationship. As we worked to put it right, we became better friends. We are stronger as a result. And then we ended the meeting with specific practical prayer for the issues raised.

May we all be fed and find ways to feed one another.

Fresh Fish Sold Here

We have the story of two brothers. One of them was Moses. He began as a liberator—today, he might be called a freedom fighter. He brought his whole people out of slavery in Egypt, and then more remarkably still, he kept them together as a people for forty years without a land of their own, simply by his faith and his leadership. Day after day, he would go up the mountain to a special place and talk with God. One day, he brought the Ten Commandments down the mountain that are the laws that now form the whole basis for Judaism and Christianity (Exodus 20:1–17).

The second man was his brother Aaron. Perhaps he was a more brilliant man, a better orator and speaker. A man who supported his brother, but he was also keen to please people. So while Moses was up the mountain, the people came to Aaron and asked, "While Moses is away, make us some gods who really help us and can give us what we need" (Exodus 32:1). Aaron listened to the people. He got them to surrender their gold jewelry. He melted it down and created a golden calf. They all shouted, "Here are your gods, O Israel" (Exodus 32:4) and they danced around their new god.

Today, we are great makers of man-made gods. There are the usual ones of money and wealth. Not bad in themselves but terrible gods. Science and the invention of computers have changed our lives giving tremendous new power and opportunities. Are they going to be more intelligent and important then human beings?

I was reminded of a little story about the fisherman who set up a little stall with a notice "Fresh Fish Sold Here." A friend came along and said, "You don't need to say 'here.' It is quite obvious you are here." The next day he came by and said, "You are not giving the fish away so you don't need the word 'sold.' Just say 'Fresh Fish.'" Another person came along and said, "A person like you would never sell fish that wasn't fresh so just put the word 'Fish.'" Finally, the next day he came along and said, "Don't bother about the word 'Fish,' we can smell it down the block!"

It may be a silly story, but it shows how little by little, we can whittle away at the foundations of our life and faith. Examination papers, in my day, often said, "Only five questions need to be attempted." I sometimes think on top of the Ten Commandments, we might find words such as "Only five of these need to be attempted or choose five you would rather have." There is a danger that we accept the parts of our faith that we like best and leave out parts that are uncomfortable or more difficult to grasp. That is what Aaron did when he substituted a man-made god that was more convenient, more comfortable to live with. It is worth asking, "Are we worshiping any graven calves?"

Making History

When I was at school, I had no use for history. In those days, what William the First, Henry the Second, or Richard the Third might have said or done couldn't mean less. I was like the small boy who when his teacher asked, "If you take 17 from 25 what is the difference?" replied, "That's right, who cares?"

Later, I had the chance to travel abroad. I went to what was then called Palestine or the Holy Land. I stood in the cave where it is thought Jesus was born. I swam in the Sea of Galilee. On foot or on the back of a donkey, I followed the tracks where Abraham travelled thousands of years ago and where Roman legions marched. I learned the fascination of history and how a handful of people in a tiny country have by their ideas and their living changed the fate of the world.

In the Bible, we read the story of Mary, the mother of Jesus. This young woman dared to say yes to a vision which was used to bring about a birth that has marked the whole of history ever since (Luke 1:46–55). Our dates are divided by BC or AD and that young woman's decision stands between.

Sometimes, we make history when we don't intend to. When I was young, most of us lived self-centered lives. The first Great War was over. It was a war to end all wars. There was a popular song that went: "I don't want to make history, I just want to make love." The trouble is that while we were living and thinking that way, we were making history. We were helping the rise of Hitler and Communism by our own indifference. The Oxford Union Debating Society passed a motion, "This house refuses to fight for king and country." Many people believe that played a big part in making Hitler decide that Britain was too decadent and pacifist to fight.

Where is the next great step in the history of the world going to be taken? Who will make history? I am convinced that there are people who will decide to lay down a style of living for the whole world. Many people today are in revolt. I hope you are rebelling against the sham and hypocrisy, the dishonesty and mismanagement. Rebel against the sloppy standards, the sex-sodden living, and the dull, dead and unimaginative spirit. If you begin to stand for something worthwhile, you will have to fight for it. You will meet tremendous opposition from the powers that be, but if you stick to your point: refuse to be coaxed or bullied out of what you honestly believe; say what you think and keep fighting, you may start to write a new page of history that will affect the whole world.

It all goes back to the story of the young woman who said yes wholeheartedly to what God was asking. It wasn't easy for Mary. She had to trust where she couldn't possibly understand. History belongs to those who say yes. There is a saying, "The world is waiting to see what God will do in and through a person wholly given to him" (Dwight L. Moody). Will you be that person?

Following a New Star

There is a story of mysterious strangers who traveled from hundreds of miles away to worship the baby Jesus. We don't know much about them. In Greek, the word "magi" is used, the root of our modern words magic and magician. It is possible they came from Persia and were followers of the prophet Zoroaster whose religion was a faith in one god with a great openness to all people. These men were evidently students of astronomy and astrology. While studying the heavens they noticed a new star. And then the most important thing, they not only recognized the star but they decided to follow it. They were seekers ready to go out into the unknown to find something new (Matthew 2:1–12).

When they got to Jerusalem, they heard that King Herod wanted to see them to discover more about this baby they were seeking. Herod felt very threatened by the idea of this child that people were calling the King of the Jews. He said to the travelers, "Go and make a careful search for the child. As soon as you find him, report to me, so that I too may go and worship him" (Matthew 2:8). But in a dream, the wise men were warned not to go back to Herod, but to return home another way.

The star led them right to the place where Jesus lay. I had a great friend, Edward Howell, an air force pilot in World War II, who was captured by the Germans and imprisoned in Greece. There was nothing there to help or encourage him. But while in prison, he gained a new knowledge of Jesus. He knew that Jesus was calling him to escape. He tells the story of how he received very clear guidance about how, when, and where to escape. Once he was out in a hostile, wild country, he followed a star which brought him through the thick of war, back safely to Britain.

Sometimes, we get a star in life, a sense of what's needed, of where to go. When you have seen a star and you have felt some personal touch with Jesus what you do next is very important. Some people feel that it is a call to give up everything, leave the life they know, and reach out for something entirely new. That great privilege came to me when I had a rather comfortable, nice job teaching in Oxford, but one day, I knew that I was called to reach out in a new and unknown way. I didn't know what it meant or where it would take me. For others of us, it is a call to pick up life as we know it but in a new and better way. It probably involves a new sense of vision and a greater concern for people. But it is easy to get caught up with the Herods of life—the various powers that be, the media, the trends of the moment, or the lures of a different life. But we are warned by God not to go back to those things but to go a different way and follow the star.

How will we be led? I hope, even at my age, that I can rediscover an adventure. I recently started keeping a diary of new things I discover each day, some star or glimpse of truth that will help me to go out with new faith and sense of adventure.

Take Away the Stone

Jesus said, "Take away the stone." This is in the amazing and mysterious story of the raising of Lazarus (John 11:1–44). The setting is a family bereavement. Every family sooner or later experiences that. This was a home and family that Jesus knew well and loved to visit. Jesus, who lived on the road without a home used to visit this home of two sisters and their brother. There was Mary, the sensitive, deeply spiritual one and Martha, the practical hostess, housekeeper, who kept the home going, and their brother Lazarus.

Then came the tragic news of Lazarus's death. This is one of the few times we are told that Jesus wept. He was deeply, deeply disturbed and troubled. Perhaps this story foreshadows Jesus's own crucifixion and death and in some way it was preparation for all that he would have to go through. In a conversation with Martha, Jesus says the words that we often repeat at the beginning of a funeral service, "I am the resurrection and the life. He that believeth in me, though he die yet shall he live" (John 11:25). Somehow, the promise of the whole resurrection were in his words, but he knew before that they could be fulfilled he would have to go through the agony of the crucifixion.

When Jesus arrives, he finds a home full of grief and suffering. Jesus asks Mary where they have laid Lazarus. Jesus says, "Take away the stone" (John 11:39) and then he commands Lazarus to come out. When they take away the stone, there is the living Lazarus. Somehow, it is easier to believe this story when we see it as a preview of the resurrection of Jesus.

I suppose for all of us at some point in our lives a stone comes across our paths to block great hurt—perhaps a wound, a hatred, a bitter memory or a sin. Jesus comes to say, "Take away the stone." When we are able to take away the stone that covers what is often unspoken or unseen, a resurrection is possible.

When I was studying at theological college, I found the principal of the college, a rather portly, shy Scotsman, very hard to get on with. He was so much of a stone that when I saw him coming, I would quickly cross to the other side of the road so I wouldn't have to meet him. One day God said to me, "Take away the stone." The stone seemed small but important. I owed him money. He had generously lent me money to buy some books when I first came to college, but over time, I had conveniently forgotten. I went to his study one morning and said, "I am sorry. Here is the money I owe you." He would never have asked for the money, but he said to himself, "Be careful of that fellow, he's not trustworthy." There was a stone. We ended up having a wonderful talk. He actually asked, "Tell me, how can I do a better job in the college?" So we spoke quite frankly about how the students felt, about how it was difficult to approach him. His response was "Let's try, with your help, to do something about this." It was a small start, but it was the beginning of a sort of resurrection.

Picking Up Your Cue

At an early performance of my first play, we had to enlist, at short notice, a new actor for a small but very important entrance at the end of the second act. As a burly worker, he had to burst into the home of a labor leader at a tense moment in an industrial dispute. He carries in the school-age daughter of the labor leader who has been knocked out in a mob at the factory gates. He lays her down on the couch and in answer to the frenzied questions of the parents he is supposed to describe in detail what has happened. Our new actor practiced carrying in the girl. He also rehearsed his fairly full and graphic speech. He never had time to put the two together. He made his entrance but dried up completely. At each frantic question, he remained completely silent. At last, with a tremendous effort, he blurted out the only words he could muster: "It's so terrible I can't speak about it!" The curtain fell on a mystified audience.

There are only three references to theater in the New Testament of the Bible. Two come from Ephesus when Paul is facing angry, rioting crowds in Corinth. To paraphrase, he says to them, "We apostles are on stage. God has made us a spectacle to the whole universe" (1 Corinthians 4:9–10). In other words we are on stage for God. One of the best things we have to offer is the ability to forget ourselves, to let ourselves go, to be so convinced of our faith that it is infectious.

If you want to know how to be onstage for God, I suggest that you take time each morning not only to pray but to listen. God will give you the cues. The cues may seem trivial, but as you pick them up, they become momentous.

We are approaching Holy Week culminating in the crucifixion of Christ and the resurrection at Easter. These historic events have been described as "the greatest drama of all time" (Matthew 27:32–56). In that wonderful and terrible story, there were just a few minor characters who managed to pick up their cue. The black passerby who helped carry Christ's cross; the women who stood faithfully by when others fled; the rough soldier who stretched up to give Christ a drink; a penitent thief who found his way at the last moment to paradise; a Centurion who made a great declaration of faith; a grieving mother and a faithful disciple. Most of the rest missed their cue. Most of the crowd beat their breasts and then went home to tea.

So in the drama unfolding in the world around us will we pick up our cue? Can we play our part however small? How do we take that vital step on stage for God? Will we be hiding in the wings, in the dark alone, or will we take the step into the light where we can play our part? It may be in the focus of our private prayers and reading, in some practical act of care, in remembering, in giving, in speaking out for what we believe in. Is there some place for each of us to pick up our cue?

A Three-Letter Word

I would like to give you just one word, and it only has three letters. It is the word "all." In the story of Easter as told by Matthew, there are four "alls." This word sums up what Easter is about. First, Jesus says, "All power is given to me by the father" (Matthew 28:18). Some tremendous power was let loose on Easter Day. We can't fully understand or explain what it was, but there was a great bursting out from the prison of death and the grave. The one thing we know for sure was that a bunch of followers, who had run away, were somehow turned into people of courage and tremendous conviction who literally began to turn the world upside down. That is power.

What has always struck me about Easter was how gentle Jesus was, how marvelously he greeted each one. He called Mary by name. He sent a special message to Peter because he knew he was feeling ashamed. To others, he just said, "Hello." It was so natural, so simple.

When our little daughter was barely three years old, my wife and I were having a time of quiet and prayer and she was making life a little bit difficult for us. I said to her rather solemnly, "Now we are trying to listen to Jesus and we are asking if he has something to say to us." She became quiet, and after quite some time, I asked, "Did Jesus say anything to you?" Right away, she replied, "He said hello." What could be a better way for a three-year-old to know Jesus?

To those who were afraid and worried Jesus said, "Peace be unto you." To a doubter, Thomas, he said, "Put your finger here… Put your hand into my side… Believe!" (John 20:27). To others, it was an invitation to come and have breakfast on the beach. And so in different simple ways, Jesus showed what it meant when he said, "All power is given to me by the father."

The next "all" is when he says "Go to all nations" (Matthew 28:19). He said this to his followers who had failed so badly, who had run away. He said, "Take on the whole world." He gave them a bigger task. And that little bunch of men and women, not outstanding, not well-known, with very little to go on humanly, began to move out into the world and share their own life changing experiences.

Then Jesus tells them, "Tell the people all things that I have commanded you" (Matthew 28:20). All the things that he has taught them. Not so much rules but standards to aim at. The very highest excellence. I am grateful for anywhere that we see excellence today. It might be the excellence of the young musicians of the year. Jesus put that standard of excellence before us. He dared to say, "Be perfect" (Matthew 5:48). He knew well that we would not succeed, but he wanted it to be our standard. To aim for it. Then you will reach higher than you ever dreamed before.

And then the last all is "always" when he says, "And lo, I am with you always, even to the end of the world" (Matthew 28:20). Jesus lives today and he can give new life to all those who want to know him. That is the greatest power in the world, but it is just the power of love. So gentle, so personal, and yet so strong, so all conquering, so wonderful.

An Honest Skeptic

Thomas was a faithful disciple of Jesus. He loved Jesus with all his heart. He was ready to die for Jesus. At one point, he said to his friends, "Come let's go with Jesus and die" (John 11:16). But he was watching like a hawk, an honest skeptic. He couldn't believe just because other people believed. He had to figure it out for himself. He was willing to express his doubts, which is a good thing for all of us to do.

After the resurrection of Jesus, Thomas was not there when Jesus appeared to his disciples. When they found him they said, "We've seen the Lord." Thomas was very skeptical and burst out, "Unless I can actually touch the wounds, I can't believe" (John 20:25–29). And then he was there and Jesus appeared. Jesus gave him what he needed, he gave him the proof he wanted. "Take my hand. Put it in the wound on my side." Thomas came out with one phrase, "My Lord and my God." Then Jesus told him, "Because you have seen me, you have believed; blessed are those who have not seen and yet have believed."

I think of Thomas as my patron saint. I was ordained on St. Thomas's Day. Anyone who dares to undertake the tremendous step and responsibility of ordination must have feelings like Thomas. As a young man of twenty-three, with little experience of the world, I was to begin my ministry in a grim area of docklands in South London where I had never been before, but where I was expected to be a spiritual leader. It seemed almost absurd, an impossible task. Then in the wonderful ordination service in Southwark Cathedral, there was a tremendous sense of the greatness of God. I knew somehow, in spite of all my inadequacy, out of my weakness comes God's strength. I have to thank God that through all the ups and downs, through the failures, and through the wonderful miracles, I don't think I have ever not been able to say with St. Thomas, "My Lord and my God."

We have been through a year of horrifying events both here and abroad. In an extraordinary way the divisions, differences, the harsh judgements, the terrible tragedy of death have all combined to bring a sense of darkness. As we approach Christmas, I think of an old saying, "It is better to light one candle than to curse the darkness." This is a good moment for all of us to light a candle of faith and action. I think one of the best candles for me was to see the children in our local school perform their Christmas play. In their last song, they sang, "From now on, it will never be the same." It was a marvelous little gleam of light in one small village. God will give us work to do, places to go, seeds to plant, light shining in the darkness.

Feed My Sheep

Jesus said to Peter, "Feed my sheep" (John 21:15–17). It is an amazing story. Peter, when asked if he was one of Christ's followers after the crucifixion, denied it three times. Later when Jesus and Peter were alone after the resurrection, Jesus didn't say a word about the denial. He didn't say, "Why did you do it?" or "I warned you, Peter." He just asked him, "Peter, do you love me?" and Peter protested, "You know, Lord, that I am your friend." Jesus simply said, "Feed my sheep." He asked this three times and each time commanded him to "Feed my sheep." Peter who had failed so terribly was given a bigger job.

What does it really mean to be that kind of shepherd? Jesus often taught by example. There is a story about two men walking back home heavy hearted and disappointed (Luke 24:13–35). We all know the experience of being down and discouraged. What did Jesus do for these two men? He walked beside them. That is something we can do for the people around us. There are times when just to come alongside, to have a cup of coffee or go for a walk together is what is needed. Just to be there can be the first important thing about being a shepherd.

God can tell you when or where to be that kind of shepherd. It is very important to do it just at the time God says. Somebody recently told me that she had the thought right out of the blue to call a friend whom she hadn't seen for a long time. She acted on the thought immediately and her friend answered, "How did you know that my brother died today?" If we are sensitive to God, we may be shown just when and where to be alongside.

Jesus did not give the two men a sermon or wonderful words of divine truth, but rather he just asked what was weighing them down. And they talked and talked pouring out their disappointment and the heaviness in their hearts. And Jesus just listened. To be this kind of shepherd you need to be a good listener. I smile to myself sometimes when someone comes in needing to talk and talk and as they leave they say, "Thank you so much. We have had such a wonderful talk and you helped me so much." I have scarcely said a word, but I have been an engaged listener.

And then there is a third thing Jesus did. They didn't know who he was, he was just a passerby, but he gave them perspective. He reminded them of God's plan right from the beginning and how it had unfolded through the ages. And then he looked forward. He put their troubles, their anxieties in a new perspective. Generally, when we are in trouble we are seeing things too narrowly, we're very absorbed by the stress and the problems of today. It is helpful to be reminded that God has been at work from the beginning and that he will be there now and in the future.

And then when Jesus said goodbye, they had to make a choice. They invited him to come in and share a meal. When they broke bread together, Jesus looked to heaven and said grace. Suddenly, they recognized who he was. It was then that they knew that the one who had walked with them on the road, listened to their story, and shared their meal would be with them to the end of time.

Those whom we accompany will also thank God for a shepherd who comes alongside and listens, who gives perspective, who gives a choice and a chance to say, "Come in."

Language Is Not a Barrier

In the church calendar, Pentecost celebrates the occasion when the Holy Spirit descended upon the Apostles and other followers of Jesus after he had left them. There were 120 of them gathered in an upper room still rather doubtful and afraid. Suddenly, there came a sound from heaven as of a rushing mighty wind, and it filled all the house where they were sitting and they were all filled with the Holy Spirit and began to speak in other languages, as the Spirit gave them utterance (Acts 2). They rushed out into the street where a crowd gathered in a festival atmosphere. They were bewildered to hear their own languages being spoken by the believers.

I think I can understand the tremendous impact that this group of convinced men and women had as they poured out what God meant to them. I remember a brilliant young Turkish woman at an international conference I attended. She was very restless and angry, and as a young Muslim, she fought against much of what she heard and she engaged in some bitter arguments. Then one evening, she chose to go to a film about a group of dockers in Brazil. It was in Portuguese, and she didn't speak one word of Portuguese. However, she sat through the film and it ended with a very moving scene of a small child, crippled from birth, who with love and faith was able to take her first steps across the room. After the film, this young woman, in floods of tears, went to her room, fell down on her knees, and gave her life to God. Language is not a barrier. She heard it in her own way because the Holy Spirit reaches each one of us at the place where we need it most.

The art of communication is a difficult one. Sometimes, we have to use little things to make the first connection. I was in India once and found myself sitting next to a very holy Indian Christian. He spoke English, but despite my best efforts, I utterly failed. I talked about the beauties of the Taj Mahal, about the church in India, about the traditions and culture of India, but as the meal continued, there was still no conversation. He seemed much too holy a person to have much to say to someone like me. And then rather casually, I said, "I see India beat Australia in cricket last week." And he said, "Yes, they did. And there is another match and everything depends on this one!" He suddenly became tremendously alive, and from that moment on in a rather extraordinary way, we were able to communicate on all sorts of subjects. It is a great art if we can discover that first moment of connection.

St. Paul tells us in the book of Acts that with the Holy Spirit "there is neither Jew nor Gentile, neither slave nor free, nor is there male and female, for you are all one in Christ Jesus" (Galatians 3:28). People were drawn together by the universal experience of God's power. So remember what it was that sent those ordinary men and women like us out into the world. Here is something that overcomes all barriers of language or point of view and brings a spirit of love, care, comfort, and strength that we need in the today's world.

A More Excellent Way

The words just before Saint Paul's great love poem are "And yet I will show you a more excellent way" (1 Corinthians 12:31). I think we would all agree that we need a more excellent way of dealing with our affairs on the world stage, in our nation, in our communities, our families, and in every single relationship.

We have recently celebrated Valentine's Day. It has blown up into a colossal commercial enterprise. Underneath the ridiculous and rather mercenary aspects, I believe there is deep in our consciousness a great longing to experience in some way a completely different spirit than the one that is around us much of the time. Romantic love is a wonderful gift. It makes the world go round and we would all be poorer without it.

And yet we know that kind of love doesn't really get down to the root of our need and our nature. Love is such a widely used word that sometimes it hardly conveys to us what it really means. Love is more than romance, it's more than feelings. Love as we heard described in St. Paul's poem is something that lasts, that goes through all the ups and downs, and when it goes through difficulties comes out stronger and more enduring than ever. And that's the kind of love which above all we long for and need. As Saint Paul so marvelously describes, "Love is patient, love is kind. It does not envy, it does not boast, it is not proud. It does not dishonor others, it is not self-seeking, it is not easily angered. It keeps no record of wrongs. Love does not delight in evil but rejoices with the truth. It always protects, always trusts, always hopes, and always perseveres. Love never fails" (1 Corinthians 13:4–7).

Author and journalist Malcolm Muggeridge and his wife Kitty were being interviewed about their long life together. Kitty was asked, "What is the great secret that has carried you through a stormy marriage, with many ups and downs and difficulties, for more than fifty years?" There was a little pause and Kitty just said, "Love." There was silence and the program ended. It was rather like a stone dropped in a pool, and in the quiet, you could almost feel the ripples spreading out and out in that one simple word, "Love."

My wife sometimes says to me when difficulty arises or there is a disappointment, "Let's go through this." It is so tempting when things are difficult to find some way of going around them. But if you go right through whatever the difficulty is, face it all, feel it all, be honest, then with God's help you can go through it together and come out stronger than ever.

And of course, in the end, it all comes down to the great fact that we love because God first loved us. He is the source of love. Sometimes, we don't know how to love or feel we cannot love a certain person. But that is the time to go to God and realize that if he loves us, he also loves that other person. We cannot love people through will power, but we can decide to act toward that other person as though we love them. That gives God a chance to come in and in time we find the feeling and strength that real love demands.

A Pattern for All Unity

It was a hot summer afternoon in the dock area of London. The trams were crowded with men going home from work. I had just managed to get one foot on the platform of a passing tram when the conductor shouted and wanted to shove me off. Suddenly, a tough-looking fellow put out a friendly hand and pulled me aboard.

"Let him on, mate," he shouted to the conductor. "This is the bloke what married me."

I had not recognized my friend as one of the countless shy and nervous bridegrooms whom I, as part of my job in a London parish, had helped into that fascinating, wonderful, sometimes fearsome state of life known as marriage.

It made me think again what a great responsibility it was to take so many marriage services. Perhaps I was lucky to have found a friend on board that tram and not an enemy who might have hissed, "Shove him off, mate. This is the bloke what married me."

And yet every marriage is a miracle. Two people each with a life and a will of their own come separately into the sanctuary. A few minutes later, they go out together–different, joined together body and soul in an eternal unity, a brand-new creation that, whatever laws, judges or experts say, can never wholly be destroyed. Like all miracles, you can't explain or analyze it even if you chose to ignore and disbelieve it. Amid all the excitement of the occasion, the one thing that really matters is what God himself has done. He has turned two into one, and for those two, life will never be the same.

The wedding service in the Christian tradition is in itself a picture of what every relationship ought to be. The two standing side by side, not looking into each other's eyes, but facing a third person in front of them. In this tradition, the third person, for all his lamentable sins and inadequacies, at that moment represents God. It is a triangle—man, woman, and God. It is an eternal triangle, a triangle with which, according to the old Bible story (Genesis 2), the whole of human history began.

These three—man, woman, and God—are the leading actors in the great drama that follows. Each has a speaking part. First God, through the minister, speaks to the man and the woman, laying down the purpose and the unbreakable condition of true marriage. Then in answer to the question, the man and woman each affirms before God their intention to join their lives in marriage. Then the man and woman speak to each other in the hauntingly beautiful words of the marriage promises, "For better or worse, for richer or poorer, in sickness or in health, till death do us part." Finally God speaks again, seals the marriage vows and crowns them with his blessing.

The world is dying for lack of unity. Maybe here in the example of marriage is a pattern for all unity—not just man and wife but labor and management, nation and nation, race and race. The eternal triangle—God, myself, and the other person. No union worth its name is going to be roses all the way. But if it is founded on a solid foundation in relationship to God, then we can know that it will be for keeps and that what God has joined together no one and no circumstances will ever be able to draw apart.

Launch Out into the Deep

I think depth is something we could all do with in a greater degree. By depth, I don't mean being terribly serious, portentous, and solemn. Some clergy and theologians make a great mistake in thinking that by being very obscure or complicated they are somehow showing great depth. No, those things are not the marks of depth. Some of the deepest people are delightful in their humor and simplicity. They have a note of reality that tolls like a deep bell. They give you a feeling that you could really talk to them and they would listen in a way that makes you feel they understand. Deep people often say less, but you remember better the things that they have said.

The story of St. Peter is a wonderful description of how Jesus trained his followers. Peter was a strange mixture. He was in some ways strong but in others weak; sometimes hasty and impetuous; sometimes cautious and hanging back; sometimes brave but at other times cowardly. Jesus, however, saw the potential in him and nicknamed him "the rock" (Matthew 16:18) because he saw a depth and a firm foundation on which he could build his church.

First of all, Jesus asked Peter for something: to lend him his boat so he could preach to the crowd gathered on the shore. It is a good start for many of us to be asked to lend or give something. Being asked for our help often establishes a relationship.

Second, Jesus offered his help when he instructed Peter to "go out and catch some fish" (John 21:4–6). Peter was the professional and expert. He thought he knew all about fishing. They had been out all night without any success. Despite feeling this was a very amateur suggestion, he agreed to go out again and Jesus went with him. It is sometimes in the realm of where we think we know best that Jesus most wants to help us.

Then the third stage is when the miracle occurs. Fishing with Jesus they caught an enormous shoal of fish, more than they could bring ashore without help. They were amazed at this extraordinary and unexpected miracle. A sense of awe was awakened in Peter. He felt small and unworthy. We will never find depth unless we discover that sense of awe. It is sometimes in our failure that we find depth.

The fourth step was when Jesus told Peter not to be afraid. He met him in his place of failure and gave him a vision of what he could be. To this fisherman he said, "Come with me, I will teach you how to catch people instead of fish" (Matthew 4:19). So Peter left his fishing business and followed Jesus. God has a different vision for each of us, something special for us to do that perhaps nobody else can.

This is an example of how our lives can be. We are all meant to have this depth of experience and understanding. We can be rocks on which, in this swirling, tempestuous world, we stand firm.

Love Is Unmistakable

The word "love" is a terribly overworked word from pop singers to theologians. To tell the truth, theologians sometimes mistreat it more than pop singers do. And yet when you see the real genuine article love is unmistakable. It isn't a pink cloud, more like a red blood transfusion. It is actually giving your blood, your life stream, so that somebody else may live.

Real love, at home for instance, is roses, but it is also a good meal cooked perfectly with whole-hearted care for the family to share. It is sugar, but it is also the salt that gives life tang and taste and brings out the best in another person. It has that great preservative quality that prevents life from going bad.

Love is romance, but it is also revolution because the most revolutionary thing there is in life is to have such a great aim and purpose that you forget all about yourself. Love, in fact, is not what happens to me, it is what happens to the other person. It is what happens when you reach out beyond yourself and lay your life down alongside somebody else.

"Greater love has no one than this: to lay down one's life for one's friends." (John 15:13). Jesus who said these words lived them, a whole life without a single thought wasted on self. It was a life given that the blind might see, the lame might walk, the dead might rise, and the guilty might be forgiven. A life given that the words in the prayer he taught us, "Thy kingdom come, thy will be done on earth as it is in heaven" (Matthew 6:10) might not just be words we repeat but a practical working reality for the whole world.

I think one of our greatest troubles today is self-centeredness and inferior thinking. It is a funny thing that now we can do and see so much more than we ever could and yet we don't seem to look further than our own noses. The world has come into our living rooms, but the problems seem so big that we don't know how to get our living out into the world. We travel abroad for our holidays, but we close our eyes to the needs of the world. We read about suffering and conflict everywhere and we think, "What can I do?" And yet all these people are our neighbors—the homeless in London, the unemployed in Scotland, the starving in Africa, the countless refugees.

First of all, we can care and feel responsible. Are we going to face life's challenges with courage and bigness of heart or are we going to run away into smallness and bitterness? Love, the real thing, begins right where we are, at home. The first step to reaching out to those in need across the world may be to venture out to our neighbor across the street.

Peak Experiences

What are peak experiences? They are not necessarily solemn, great occasions. They sometimes come quite unexpectedly, by surprise. They may even seem to be little things, but when they come we know and we say to ourselves, "This is it. This is what life is all about. This is something to treasure and never forget." I remember when I was fifteen years old, hearing a big symphony live for the first time. It was so exciting, it shot me right out of my seat and it took several days before I came down to earth. And I remember thinking, *Well, if life's like that, life will never be the same again.* Are there moments when you have said, "Yes, this is what life is all about?" Perhaps you were all by yourself on a starlit night when you became aware of the vast shape, meaning, and infinity of the universe. It might be when you first fell in love. Or it may be when you saw something that was absolutely perfect. The first time I watched the famous ballet dancer Margot Fonteyn dance, I said to myself, "This is a peak experience I'll never forget!"

There are times when all of us have had a glimpse of a vision beyond our understanding, far greater than we realize, and we think to ourselves, "My, if the whole world could be like that," and then we have had to come right down to earth with all its frustrations and disappointments. But then, that is the whole point, that we take with us into the world that vision that we had in our peak experience.

As a young man in Oxford, I was kneeling in a rather perfunctory way at the beginning of the service in the university church. Suddenly, the whole wonder of the reality of God swept over me in a new way and I knew Christ was real. I knew that the whole meaning of my life was to serve him. After the service, I sailed down the road with my feet hardly touching the ground. It was a wonderful peak experience that I often try to recall. Was it true? The mountaintop experiences are real but the down-to-earth ones are also real. Our job is to bring the two together and to live to make them one.

When you are first ordained as a young clergyman, it is a tremendous peak experience. For me, it was being in the glory and wonder of Southwark Cathedral, the solemn service, and then the experience of preaching in a cathedral for the first time. This was followed by two wonderful years working in this very poor part of South London. I found myself in what were once gracious houses that now housed eight families with children sharing one bathroom, going to the hospital, and seeing young people dying of tuberculosis, for which there was no real cure then, going to the asylum, going to the prison, going to all the parts of a busy parish. And yet it was the happiest, most wonderful time for me, thrilling because now I realized how to take that vision, peak experience of being up the mountain and try, as best I could, to live it out amid all the harshness, the humor, and delight of a great crowded London parish.

The Green-Eyed Monster

Jealousy is not a thing that most of us like to admit or own up to. And yet I think if we are honest all of us have had these jealousies at some time in our lives. Somebody else got there first. Somebody else got more than his share. Somebody else got the credit when I had done most of the work. Most of these twinges of jealousy we get over and forget, but every now and then, it becomes more than a twinge, it becomes a real poison. It can become a cancer. It can drive us round the bend and even lead to death.

Shakespeare wrote an amazing play, *Othello*, about a seed of jealousy and suspicion that was cleverly fostered by a rival until it became a terrible possessing madness. Othello, a great man, is so possessed with the poison of jealousy that he murders his wife and the story ends in tragedy. There is a line in the play that I often remember, "O beware, my lord, of jealousy; it is the green-eyed monster."

Now, what about us? The first person that jealousy hurts is us, not the other person. It has a way of turning us against ourselves.

Many years ago I had the chance to know Artur Rodziński, an outstanding conductor of the New York Philharmonic. While he was away at his country farm for the summer, a younger conductor, a very promising young man, took on the orchestra and they gave a series of outdoor concerts in a New York stadium. One night, my friend decided to listen to one of the concerts on the radio to see how the young man was doing. The concert had already begun. Very soon, my friend began to get very excited and commented, "This is wonderful, this is magnificent. This young man is a genius. This young man will rise to the top."

You saw the frenzy of jealousy begin to take hold and he started pacing the room. At the end of the symphony, he was in an appalling state of jealousy. Then there was absolute silence. Were people so impressed they couldn't even applaud? Then a voice came on the radio and said. "Owing to rain the concert was cancelled, and we have heard a recording of the symphony conducted by Artur Rodziński." He had spent the evening in a frenzy of jealousy of himself!

We are all different. Different gifts, different qualities. There is only one great absolute of equality, and that is that we are all a part of God's family. Whoever we are, we share fully in his love. Everyone is precious, unique, and a part of that family. It is God's wish, not that we should all be alike, but that each of us has a chance to be more what God wants us to be. This becomes possible when we recognize jealousy and deal with it. The solution is in our relationship to God himself.

Nations, individuals, political parties, and yes, churches too, spend an awful lot of time eying one another with suspicion, with jealousy and sometimes almost a frenzy of hatred. Would that we could all find our place as part of God's family so that the tragedies that come from the madness of jealousy might be put aside and give us a chance to discover his perfect plan.

The Lost Is Found

I am a terrible person for losing things—that important document, those unanswered letters, that precious photograph or magazine lent and not returned, and so on. Somehow, losing things is worse than just being without them. It creates in me a kind of restless, distracted feeling. I'll settle down to some work and then I feel I must go and look in the wastepaper basket in case I threw it away or worse search the trash can outside. Losing things brings a horrible sense of emptiness. It helps a great deal to pray and I've proved that again and again. And then it often happens that you have the wonderful experience of finding it. I often find what was lost right at the place where I first started looking and where it was supposed to be all along. But I had the wrong idea of what I was looking for. I thought it was blue, but it is really red, I thought it was large but it was smaller. But there it is. You have great joy in finding what had been lost. You want to tell other people, "It is found!"

I remember a good many years ago coming back to our house and seeing a delightful puppy running all over our lawn. With some difficulty, we caught him and brought him in to our house. We had no idea where he belonged. Then I had the thought to go out into the road. I saw a car slowly turn into the farm opposite. I followed it and there was a lady searching for something. I said, "I know what you are looking for. He is quite safe, he is in our house." Sometime later, this same neighbor came to our house and asked, "Will you pray? Will you pray hard because I've lost a very special bracelet?" She added, "I think you've got a hot line to God!"

We did pray, and two or three days later, she returned, "You are not praying hard enough! We still have not found it." And so with her, we prayed again. A little later came the good news that the bracelet had been found.

Jesus gave us two marvelous little stories on this theme. One about the shepherd who lost just one sheep from his flock, but he goes looking for it and keeps searching until it is found. Then he lays it on his shoulders rejoicing. When he gets home, he calls his friends together and tells them the good news, "What was once lost is now found." The second story is about the woman who lost her precious silver piece. She lights a candle and sweeps in the dark corners of her house and searches until she finds it. She runs out into the street and calls to her friends, "I have found what I was looking for!" Then Jesus dares to say, "In the same way there is joy in heaven over one sinner, one person who repents and comes home again" (Luke 15:3–10).

Perhaps too often we think of us finding God and the joy we get when, after perhaps a huge sense of loss, of something missing, we have found the reality of God in our hearts. That is wonderful, but it isn't what Jesus was talking about in these stories. He was talking about the joy of God himself, the joy in heaven, when God actually finds one of us. It is wonderful to find something, but it is far more wonderful to find someone.

The Question of Place

Jesus was interested in weddings. He was interested in people and he knew that weddings are full of the stuff of human drama. Hopes, fears, love, heartache, and tension are all there. Jesus knew about all the things that go on behind the scenes and the little things that can blow up into big storms, the refreshments that run out, the guests who don't appear, the bridesmaids who fall asleep, the fellow who is not properly dressed.

Then there is the seating, the question of place. If you have ever had to seat a big banquet, you know the many pitfalls. Will so-and-so fit with so-and-so? Will so-and-so be offended if they are not at the top table? Many a happy occasion has been ruined on the issue of place.

But we are all involved in questions of place. Jesus never says that place does not matter. In one parable, he tells us, "Choose the lowest place" (Luke 14:10). That is not necessarily where you belong, but until you are willing to be nothing, God may not be able to give you anything. Until you stop grabbing, God may not start giving. People who all their lives are on the make, on the climb, sometimes end up with no place at all; empty people in an empty world. We must be willing to serve others, to wash people's feet, get out of the rat-race and stop thinking about our rights, our hurt feelings. You may learn something you have never learned before.

But then Jesus might also say, "Friend, go up higher" (Luke 14:10). It may be just as bad, just as selfish to hog the bottom place as to scramble for the top. Some of us love a nice, cozy, inconspicuous place when God is actually saying, "Take on more. Think bigger."

I grew up in England as the son of a minister, not a wealthy home but protected and comfortable. Like my father and three brothers, I studied to be a minister. During my studies, I visited the Middle East. The current conflicts were just beginning. A friend of mine was shot and nearly killed. It was a seething pot. There was a lot of pettiness, of backbiting and real hatred. I realized that as a Christian minister-to-be, I had nothing to offer. I returned to Oxford feeling a failure. "I can't face it. It is too big." In Jerusalem, I had accomplished nothing. I had failed utterly and felt like giving up.

Then in an encounter with a friend in Oxford, he reminded me that "God has a plan. You have a part" (Jeremiah 29:11). As a theological student, I was familiar with the idea, but suddenly, it made sense. This life isn't an accident with one thing after another. There is a plan. Not a static, fixed plan but a creative developing plan unfolding every day. "You have a part and a place." If you do not accept and fulfill your part, there will be something essential missing in the world. God said to me, "I gave you a job to do and you failed. But I am going to give you a bigger job. Go up higher. I will show you how." And so day by day, listening to God, I began to discover my place. It is not a question of up or down. The important thing is obedience.

The Salt of the Earth

Jesus said to his followers, "You are the salt of the earth" (Matthew 5:13). I don't think he was handing out compliments, telling them that they were wonderful, superior to all other people around. I don't think he was just addressing then individually, but he looked around at the little band of followers and reminded them of what their role in life was to be. "You are the salt of the earth." You have a special job to do. Be sure you do it.

Salt, above all, is a preservative. Before the days of fridges, freezers, and the like, salt played a great part in the preservation of food. Without a good dose of preservatives to keep it fresh, it tends to decay and die. The body also needs salt. There is a great tendency to corruption running right through the whole of life. Never more than now we see the need in family life, we see it in mindless, hideous violence and the constant down drag that afflicts us all. We need something to preserve us and keep us clean.

William Wilberforce became a fresh young member of Parliament at the age of twenty-one. Wilberforce was socially popular and a desired presence at parties. Suddenly, he was struck by the power of God and his whole life was turned around. That didn't drive him out of politics, but it sent him more deeply into the greatest corruption of his time. God laid upon him a great salty task in a very corrupt society. He was led to tackle the vested interests of the trans-Atlantic slave trade. Most people were not aware and fewer still cared. It just went on. The ships went out laden with cheap trinkets and returned full of spices, sugar, rum, and cotton. Few knew what happened in between: the kidnappings, the awful deaths, the terrible mutilations, the drownings, and the selling of the slaves. Wilberforce felt it was laid upon him to end the trading of slaves and then slavery itself. It took a lifetime to have slavery declared illegal throughout the British possessions. Wilberforce didn't do it all alone. He was at the center of a group of men and women, some in politics, some in business, some clergy who met together to try to be the salt in a corrupt age and to bring a new wholesomeness to life.

A salty relationship is not a cozy, sentimental relationship. A salty relationship has its humor; it has its occasional sting of truth. It has the unexpected and imaginative. Salt after all brings out the taste. You don't want a diet of salt alone. It would be poisonous. Our job is not to stand out or draw attention to ourselves. Not to be pious or constantly moralizing. Somehow, true salt in a relationship helps the other person to bring forth their best and grow closer to what God wants them to be.

As a very confused young man in a certain amount of trouble, I sought counsel from such a wise and salty friend. I arrived ready to talk a lot about myself. But as we began, he asked, "Alan, would you straighten that picture on the wall?"

I moved it, and he said, "No, further, further. Not that way, the other way."

It took a long time before I got the picture hanging right. My friend responded, "That's better. Now it is hanging straight. You know I hate to be in a room with something that isn't straight."

We talked after that about all sorts of other things, but I always remember that salty conversation which helped bring a new savor to my life.

The Time to Decide

"You have not chosen me, but I have chosen you" (John 15:16). Who does the choosing in our lives? Of course most of us would say, "I do." But it is only in a limited sense that any of us can choose our lives. If people are in difficult circumstances, perhaps very hard up or unemployed or maybe they are working flat out pressed by responsibilities almost too crushing to bear, it isn't always easy to feel we chose this life.

In a marriage, it is sometimes the husband who does the choosing, at other times, it is the wife. I once heard a man say, "When we got married, we agreed that I would make all the big decisions and my wife would make the small ones." When asked how it was going, he responded, "So far, there have not been any big decisions."

We are each responsible for the choices we make. It is we who have to decide. We cannot pass the buck or blame others or circumstances. A young man used to come and see me when I was a chaplain in Oxford. He loved to discuss and debate about faith and religion. Day after day, night after night, he'd drop in and bring up the same discussions and arguments, back and forth, back and forth. I finally lost my patience and I said to him, "Hugh, if you have anything more to say on this subject, say it tonight because I'm never going to discuss this with you again. We've covered the ground so many times, I have nothing more to add. I hope we can remain friends, but this is the end of the discussion."

He got rather indignant and red in the face. He jumped out of his chair and said, "Well, of course if that is the way you feel, good night," and he left.

I spent a horrible night thinking I had made a mistake. But early the next morning, there was a knock at the door. He popped his head in and said, "I just wanted to tell you that I have decided God is in charge of my life."

He needed that jolt to bring him from the place of endless discussion and delay to the place of decision. There comes a moment when not to decide is to say no. So it is with our relationship with God. We decide, we choose, it's our responsibility.

But that is only half the story. Before ever we decided, God had chosen us. It is later on as we look back on life that we realize God's guiding hand has been there all the time. We have taken little steps, taken decisions, yet behind it all has been God's wonderful choosing. Often, when you are chosen for something you feel God has made a great mistake. Moses, the great leader in the Bible, first said, "No, Lord, you've got the wrong man" (Exodus 3:11). Jeremiah protested, "Oh no, Lord, not me. I am much too young and I've got no courage" (Jeremiah 1:6). And so I think at times when we have a call to do something or be something we are tempted to say, "Not me, Lord." And yet so much depends on our willingness to say, "Yes." Some people turn away and end up in the wilderness. Others are so busy, pre-occupied, and self-centered that they are chosen but they never hear the call. When we hear our call, may we be ready to say, "Yes."

Where There Is No Vision

"Where there is no vision the people perish" (Proverbs 29:18.) If you look at more modern translations of the Bible, they give a different version: "Where there is no vision the people break loose, get out of hand or run wild." Looking at the world today, we see so many examples of violence and brutality. Perhaps when we run wild and break loose, these are signs that we have lost our vision. We don't know where to go. We don't know what it is all about. We don't have any sense of purpose. Sometimes, out of sheer boredom or frustration or sense of nothingness, we break out in all kinds of ways.

I am thinking about "seeing" and how that is a way of navigating with God and communicating with him. I was grateful to have a good friend called Peter Warnett who worked in our garden for many years and who introduced me to a whole new world. I think that as a young man, I was very self-centered, selfish, and bent on my own affairs. The lovely lanes around where we lived were places for me to try out my motorbike. There were tennis parties and nice gardens to sit in and study, but I had practically no idea of the whole wonderful world of nature and the thousands of living creatures around me. I am still a great ignoramus, but Peter Warnett opened my eyes and I began to learn a little bit about the countryside. He used to say, "The thing about the country is that it is all there for you to find. Everything is free. You must know how to look. You have eyes to see."

Now I wonder in the same way, if we go right through our lives eating, drinking, working, sleeping, but we don't give a thought to the amazing world that is all around us, perhaps we miss seeing the world of the spirit. It is closer than we can touch. Either we have got eyes to see or we go through life blind and we never realize that the living God is right here in our midst.

What sort of vision can we expect from God? It comes in different ways to every person. Sometimes, it means we have to see ourselves more clearly before we can see other people clearly. So many of us are blind to what is going on right around us, even in our own homes.

Two men are working on a building site and you say to one, "What are you doing?"

He says, "I am heaving stones and mortaring, plastering and going slow so that I get more overtime."

And you ask the next man, "What are you doing?"

He says, "I am building a cathedral."

He had a vision. He knew why he was doing what he was doing.

Where there is no vision, we just get out of hand and perish. Where there is vision, life can be full of discovery, amazement, and wonder.

Which Son Are You?

There is great pain in losing things and great joy in finding them. Jesus spoke of lost sheep and lost coins. But perhaps the most beautiful and wonderful story ever told is the parable Jesus tells about a lost son (Luke 15:11–32). This story gives us a lot to think about.

First of all, the younger son demands, "Give me my rights!" He wants his inheritance now. How often we hear that all around the world. "I want it now." Credit is often sold to us as "taking the waiting out of wanting." The father grants his request because he knows it is the only way that the boy will learn. He wants what many of us want—to find himself, to be on his own, to be his own man. Well, the story tells us that everything goes wrong as he squanders his wealth in wild living. Only when he reaches the bottom and is living with the pigs in their sty does he come to his senses and says, "I will go back home and I will ask my father to make me one of his servants." To come to one's senses is a vital stage for all of us as we discover the real meaning in life. A friend of mine who has worked with drug addicts knows that the first important step on the road to recovery is when they can say, "I am responsible." Blame cannot be placed anywhere else—friends, pushers, parents, or society at large. This is the only place where the long journey back can begin.

And then the father sees the young man in the distance on the road home looking weary and dejected. The father runs to the son, throws his arms around him and kisses him. He does not even wait to hear what the son has to say. If you are a father and that is your son or daughter coming home then you run. The son says to him, "Father, I have sinned against heaven and against you. I am no longer worthy to be called your son." But the father orders a celebration and declares, "This son of mine was dead and is alive again, he was lost and is found."

And then there is the other son. Rudyard Kipling wrote, "Perhaps the reason why the younger son left home was the older son." Perhaps he was difficult to live with. Maybe it was hard to be his younger brother. He was very hardworking, very correct, very obedient, but very self-righteous and hard. He hears the wonderful celebration, feasting, music, and dancing going on. The angry older brother will not go in. The father, who loves the older brother equally, comes out to talk to him. He says, "Everything I have is yours. You are mine. But we have to celebrate and be glad, because this brother of yours was dead and is alive again; he was lost and is found."

This is not the story of one son but two. But what it is really about, more than either of the two sons, is the one loving father. He is the central character in the whole story and at its heart it is about the way he treats each one of his sons.

And now I will end with a question for all of us, "Which of the two sons are you?"

Why Are You So Fearful?

Fear. Everyone has it at some point. Talk to people who have won special distinction for bravery or who have done great acts of courage and they nearly always tell you, "Yes. I was scared stiff. I had fear, but there was something else too."

There is a story of Jesus in a boat with some of his disciples on the Sea of Galilee (Mark 4:35–41). Jesus was exhausted and fell asleep. Then a sudden, violent storm came up. Though they were experienced sailors they became afraid. In a panic, the disciples shook Jesus awake and said, "Don't you care that we might perish?"

Jesus replied, "Why are you so fearful?"

Then he spoke to the storm and calmed it.

Fear, in one way or another, hits us all. It can come suddenly like a huge storm or terrifying event. But it can also come creeping up on you at 2 o'clock in the morning when it's all quiet and you are alone. You start by imagining things and then it escalates until you are full of fear.

How do you deal with that fear? What is it that takes us right through the fear and out the other side? It helps sometimes to name your fear. Don't spread your fears to everyone around you because fears are infectious, but it often helps to find a trusted friend and unpack the fear that has you in its grip. It may be as simple as worry about what others will think of you or that you've made a big mistake or that you'll make a wrong decision and risk a relationship; or you are afraid of standing up for what you know is right. Whatever it is, name it and look it in the face. Very often in an extraordinary way it will melt away. A friend of mine used to say, "Whatever you fear, draw near, it will probably disappear."

Often, you can go through the fear before you have to actually face it. There is a saying, "Leave nothing to chance and then leave everything to God." If you have something difficult to do, try to think it through as carefully as possible, and when you have done that, you can leave it absolutely to God. It is not always given in advance, but perhaps you have to face an exam, an interview, or even an operation, when the actual moment comes, there is a great sense of calm and you know there is a power with you that will carry you through.

But there is something more. Fear can actually be a friend. We need a certain amount of fear. A child who touches a hot stove once learns through fear a lesson for life. We need this in all sorts of ways to learn how to live and how not to live. Without any fear, we would be in danger of being fools. There is quite a different kind of fear—a fear of the Lord. That may sound like an old-fashioned idea. Perhaps awe is a better word than fear. We need a sense of the greatness and wonder of God and to know that if we go against him there are consequences. It's a fact that if we lose our fear of God we can get lost in the fears of one another and of what the future might bring. In the end we lose fear when we have something stronger than fear, "Perfect love casts out fear" (1 John 4:18).

Will It Last?

Sometimes when we experience a spiritual awakening, a fresh burst of faith and decide to follow Jesus other people come along and say, "This is fine, it is wonderful, but will it last?" It is a rather foolish question really. What would a proud mother think if she brought home a beautiful baby only to be faced with people asking, "This is fine, it is wonderful, but will it last?" Any sound healthy baby will last and it will grow and thrive if we do our part. Any child needs certain things. It needs air, food, and exercise every day.

As people new to faith, we need air. The life with God is as natural and as constant as breathing. It is breathing in and breathing out. We tell God the things that are on our hearts. That is the breathing out. Then we breathe in as we are quiet and let God tell us what he wants of us. We breathe out as we give God our time and talent, our money, our lives and then we breathe in again as God gives us his love, his forgiveness, his strength, his wisdom. We breathe in as he tells us what he wants us to do and we breathe out as we obey and serve him. If there is one thing that is going to make the spirit of new faith last and grow, it is the early morning lung stretching before all the business of the day when we breathe in the gifts of God and breathe out the longings, the shameful things and the fears in our hearts. It is as normal and necessary as breathing is for a living soul.

Then there is food. There are many kinds of food that we badly need. There are the books we read. For many of us that may be the Bible. We are all travelers on a journey and the Bible is the story of those who have traveled that way ahead of us. It tells of the heights they have scaled and the depths to which they have fallen and what we can learn from both. We will find other books that introduce us to those who served God down through history such as a young man named St. Augustine, a courageous girl named Joan of Arc, or a rebel known as St. Francis, and other great men and women. It will deepen your thinking and understanding. Pay attention to what is happening in the world around you and be on the lookout for where God is at work and what part you may be meant to play.

Then we need a daily work-out—to take what God has given us and work it out in our lives and in the lives of our family and community. If you want to keep an experience fresh, you have to give it away. A thermometer is a useful thing. It will tell you what the temperature is around you. But it is a cheerless thing on a winter day to huddle around a thermometer. You need a radiator. We need to decide whether we are going to be thermometers accurately reflecting the temperature around us or are we going to be radiators that add warmth and change the status quo. If we plan every day to change our environment, then that environment will not be able to change us. That is our daily exercise.

If we are faithful, we will be given everything we need to carry us through the tasking, triumphant, and tremendous days ahead.

The Eternal Friendship

Excerpts from the last chapter of Alan
Thornhill's book, *Best of Friends.*

I have come to the realization that for me every friendship has
become a three-cornered affair. Christ is the unseen friend in every
relationship.

Christ's friendship starts from the very first moment of our lives
and goes on to the very end. It is in one sense a natural, easy, and
enjoyable friendship. Christ was a friend of publicans and sinners. I
often think that is what angered the Pharisees more than anything
else was not that Jesus went to the publicans and sinners to save their
souls, but that he seemed to enjoy them and felt at home at their
table.

I sensed Christ's friendship to me as a small child. Nobody can
overestimate a childhood experience of Christ's friendship learnt
from parents. I can see myself still, not more than three or four years
old, shouting with glee the words of the song, "Trust and obey, for
there's no other way to be happy with Jesus, than to trust and obey."

The whole thing became real in a new way after living in the
Holy Land. On the surface, it was a peaceful spot. I loved it all and
spent many hours walking or riding a donkey, roaming the countryside around Jerusalem. Somehow I felt closer to Christ when I was
jostled and pushed by crowds, bemused by the noise of bargainers
and money changers, smelling the smells, moved by human need
and tragedy, the blind, the lame, the children in the gutter, as well as

travelers from other countries. It was all in Christ's world. He knew it and I came to know it too.

But he was not yet my friend. I came home deeply disillusioned, not with Christ, but with my own lack of a faith adequate to deal with the rising passions of the Middle East. It was back in Oxford in St. Mary's Church, quite suddenly and simply that I let Jesus become my friend. I had not thought at the time that I was a miserable sinner. It was just an amazing discovery that Jesus was offering me everything and above all his friendship for life.

The friendship with Christ that followed has grown over the years. It is an infinite process of discovery. For me, the most precious hour of the day is the first hour of the morning. Whether it is in the cold darkness of the winter when, huddled in a blanket, fortified with a cup of coffee, you face a new day, or amid the glory of spring, you awake to the dawn chorus of birds, and a burst of new life in nature sets your mind and senses soaring or sitting with a paper and pen to note down those quiet, urgent often elusive thoughts that the Holy Spirit gives any honest listener. Every day can begin with fresh discoveries of friendship with Christ. Lose that precious morning hour and you may have lost the day. Seize it before phone calls, letters, newspapers, and engagements come crowding in. Life that day can have special meaning and a genuine sense of adventure.

Lately, I have been keeping a diary entitled *Discoveries*. Almost every day there is something to record, a fresh look at nature or the world, some new insight or encounter with a person, something in a book or conversation, even a really good joke. Maybe it is a spark of inspiration, a new vision of God. Sometimes I awake with the name of a person beating on my brain. Sure enough I may discover that person is in special need. Often, Christ is there with a familiar "Fear not. Go in peace."

As you listen, you also encounter the revolutionary Christ pledged to go on to the end of the line to bring a dying world to its true destiny. If that is his business, then as his friend, it must also be mine. It means total commitment. No holds barred, nor private reservations, no easy options, no room for a crumb of personal self-satisfaction, or the tiniest corner of a private life of my own but everything given for ever.

Every day, I use a prayer that was taught me by the actor, Bernard Miles, "Oh, God, please help me to help you today." Christ trusts us to be his hands, his feet, his mouth, part of his plan.

---

* *Best of Friends* published by Marshall Pickering, 1986

About the Author

Alan Thornhill was an English priest and playwright. Educated at Oxford University, he was ordained in Southwark Cathedral in 1929 and served in a large London parish before returning to his Oxford College as a Fellow and Chaplain in the 1930s. Curiosity about life and a wide range of interests, a deep love of people and an eagerness to discover new things led him unexpectedly to write his first play, *The Forgotten Factor*, in America during World War II. The play ran on Broadway and in Washington, DC, before arriving in London's West End. It was translated into sixteen languages and was seen on all continents. Over the next three decades, many other plays followed, including *Mr. Wilberforce, MP*; *Bishop's Move*; *Ride! Ride!* and *Sentenced to Life*. His books include *Best of Friends* that traces his own spiritual discoveries made through a variety of friendships. He retired to Sussex where he served in a small country parish until his death in 1988. He was married to an American, Barbara van Dyke.

Discoveries Along the Way with Alan Thornhill is a book of short reflections taken from his sermons. They were edited by his daughter, Susan Corcoran, who lives with her husband, Rob, in Austin, Texas. She is the mother of three sons, Neil, Mark, and Andrew, who all had the chance to know their grandfather and are proud of his legacy.

CPSIA information can be obtained
at www.ICGtesting.com
Printed in the USA
LVHW111944160921
697992LV00003B/104